DEC 0 3 2018

D1408505

WITHDRAWN FROM LIBRARY

WHAT ARE VITAMINS?

CORONA BREZINA

Britannica®
Educational Publishing

IN ASSOCIATION WITH

ROSEN
EDUCATIONAL SERVICES

Published in 2019 by Britannica Educational Publishing (a trademark of Encyclopædia Britannica, Inc.) in association with The Rosen Publishing Group, Inc.
29 East 21st Street, New York, NY 10010

Copyright © 2019 The Rosen Publishing Group, Inc. and Encyclopædia Britannica, Inc. Encyclopædia Britannica, Britannica, and the Thistle logo are registered trademarks of Encyclopædia Britannica, Inc. All rights reserved.

Distributed exclusively by Rosen Publishing.
To see additional Britannica Educational Publishing titles, go to rosenpublishing.com.

First Edition

Britannica Educational Publishing
J. E. Luebering: Executive Director, Core Editorial
Mary Rose McCudden: Editor, Britannica Student Encyclopedia

Rosen Publishing
Kathy Kuhtz Campbell: Senior Editor
Nelson Sá: Art Director
Nicole Russo-Duca: Series Designer and Book Layout
Cindy Reiman: Photography Manager
Nicole DiMella: Photo Researcher

Library of Congress Cataloging-in-Publication Data

Names: Brezina, Corona, author.
Title: What are vitamins? / Corona Brezina.
Description: New York: Britannica Educational Publishing, in Association
with Rosen Educational Services, 2019. | Series: Let's find out! Good health | Audience: Grades 1–4. | Includes bibliographical references and index.
Identifiers: LCCN 2017051001| ISBN 9781538303061 (library bound) | ISBN 9781538303078 (pbk.) | ISBN 9781538303085 (6 pack)
Subjects: LCSH: Vitamins in human nutrition—Juvenile literature. |
Vitamins—Juvenile literature. | Nutrition—Juvenile literature.
Classification: LCC QP771 .B74 2019 | DDC 613.2/86—dc23
LC record available at https://lccn.loc.gov/2017051001

Manufactured in the United States of America

Photo credits: Cover, back cover, pp. 1, 14, interior pages background Evan Lorne/Shutterstock.com; p. 4 Mat Hayward/Shutterstock.com; p. 5 Tetra Images/Brand X Pictures/Getty Images; p. 6 Encyclopædia Britannica, Inc.; p. 7 PattyK/Shutterstock.com; p. 8 Kateryna Kon/Shutterstock.com; p.9 Monkey Business Images/ Shutterstock.com; p. 10 elenabsl/Shutterstock.com; p. 11 Mike Kemp/Blend Images/Getty Images; p. 12 Designua/Shutterstock.com; p. 13 bitt24/Shutterstock.com; p. 15 Westend61/Getty Images; p. 16 Kenneth Batelman/Ikon Images/Getty Images; p. 17 Alexander Raths/Shutterstock.com; p. 18 Nastya Pirieva /Shutterstock.com; p. 20 Ryan DeBerardinis/Shutterstock.com; p. 21 BIOPHOTO ASSOCIATES/PRI/Science Source/Getty Images; p. 22 Jeff Rotman/Photolibrary/Getty Images; p. 23 Wellcome Collection/CC BY 4.0; p. 24 Evg Zhul/Shutterstock.com; p. 25 Justin Sullivan/Getty Images; p. 26 Jupiterimages/Pixland/Thinkstock; p. 27 U.S. Food and Drug Administration; p. 28 Sheila Fitzgerald/Shutterstock.com; p. 29 Africa Studio /Shutterstock.com.

Contents

INTRODUCING VITAMINS

Vitamins are nutrients that humans need to grow, reproduce, and be healthy. They help to keep the systems of the body working properly. Each vitamin has specific roles to play. Many processes in the body require several vitamins. Too much or too little of one vitamin can interfere with the function of another.

Scientists have identified thirteen vitamins that are **essential** for good health: A, C, D, E, and K, plus eight B vitamins. (Many vitamins have scientific names as

Vitamins are very important for keeping people healthy. Vitamins regulate many different functions of the body.

A balanced diet of a variety of foods can provide the vitamins needed for good health.

VOCABULARY

Things that are **essential** are so important that they have to be included.

well as their letter names.) Most of these vitamins can be obtained through a healthy diet filled with a variety of foods, including plenty of fruits and vegetables. Two vitamins—D and K—are made in the human body. Vitamins are needed in only small amounts, but a lack of any essential vitamin can cause health problems.

VITAMINS AND THE HUMAN BODY

Vitamins function as tools in the body. Although vitamins are not an energy source, they help to convert food's nutrients—carbohydrates, fats, and proteins—into energy. Vitamins also play a role in building tissues and regulating chemical activities.

There are two groups of vitamins: water soluble and fat soluble. Water-soluble vitamins include the B vitamins and vitamin C. They dissolve in water. The body stores a small amount of

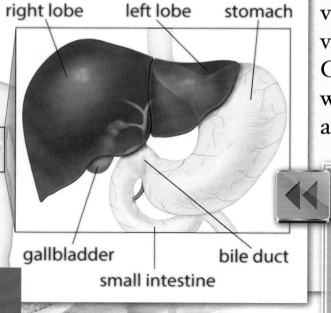

right lobe   left lobe   stomach

gallbladder   bile duct

small intestine

The liver is a large organ located next to the stomach. The liver stores nutrients such as vitamins and minerals.

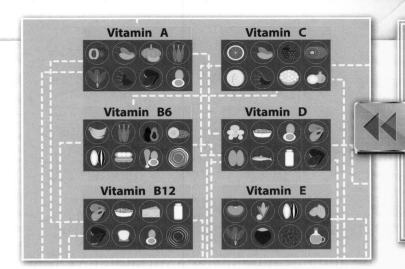

Vitamin A
Vitamin C
Vitamin B6
Vitamin D
Vitamin B12
Vitamin E

Vitamins can be obtained from a wide variety of plant and animal foods, making it easy to meet daily requirements.

water-soluble vitamins, but it gets rid of most of those it does not use. Because of that, people must get a steady supply of those vitamins. Fat-soluble vitamins include A, D, E, and K. They do not dissolve in water and are mostly stored in the body's fat and liver.

THINK ABOUT IT

Why might it be useful for the body to store some vitamins?

Different amounts of each vitamin are recommended for men and women at different life stages. A value called the recommended dietary allowance (RDA) is the daily amount of a nutrient that meets the needs of most healthy people.

VITAMIN A

Vitamin A is a fat-soluble vitamin that is also called retinol. It is very important for good vision. Vitamin A also supports several other parts and functions of the body. These include the reproductive system, bone and tissue growth, and organs such as the heart and kidneys. In addition, vitamin A helps the body's immune system to fight off infections.

There are two types of dietary sources of vitamin A. Preformed vitamin A is found in animal products, such as liver, fish oils, dairy products, and eggs. Plants do

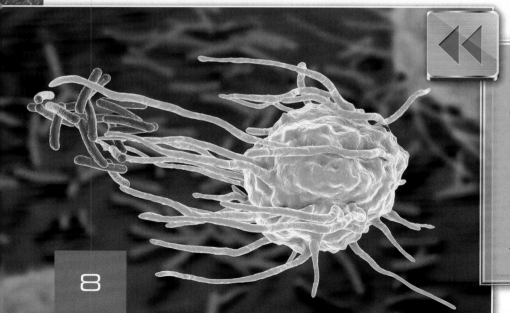

A cell (*near right*) produced by the immune system prepares to attack and destroy harmful tuberculosis bacteria.

THINK ABOUT IT

A lot of orange vegetables and fruits contain beta carotene, which is turned into vitamin A in the body. Do you think any of your favorite vegetables or fruits are good sources of vitamin A?

not contain vitamin A, but some plant foods do provide vitamin A precursors. These are chemicals that the body can convert into vitamin A. Vitamin precursors are also called provitamins. Beta carotene, for example, is a vitamin A precursor found in carrots and other vegetables.

Carrots are a source of beta carotene, which is a chemical that the body converts into vitamin A.

VITAMIN C

Vitamin C is a water-soluble vitamin also called ascorbic acid. It plays an important role in building and repairing connective tissue that is found in muscles, fat, and joints. For this reason, vitamin C helps to heal wounds. Vitamin C also supports the immune system and helps the body to absorb iron, an important mineral. In addition, vitamin C is an **antioxidant** that works to protect the body's cells from damage. People sometimes take extra vitamin C to fight off a cold, but scientific research has found that doing so is not very useful.

RDA
RECOMMENDED
DIETARY
ALLOWANCE

60 mg

60 mg

BELL PEPPER
80.4 mg

KALE
120 mg

KIWI
92.7 mg

BROCCOLI
89.2 mg

TOMATOES
13.7 mg

VITAMIN
C

CHEMICAL STRUCTURE

ASCORBIC ACID

FUNCTIONS

IMMUNE SYSTEM
MANTEINANCE

TEETH AND
GUM HEALTH

MANTAINS
HEALTHY SKIN

ANTIOXIDANT

Many fruits and vegetables are excellent sources of vitamin C.

VOCABULARY

An **antioxidant** is a substance that opposes oxidation—reactions made easier by oxygen. In the body, antioxidants help to prevent harmful reactions.

Vitamin C is found in many fruits and vegetables, especially cantaloupe, citrus fruits, vegetables in the cabbage family, peppers, sweet potatoes, and leafy green vegetables. They yield the most vitamin C when eaten raw and fresh. Cooking and long storage can reduce amounts of vitamin C in fruits and vegetables.

Fruits such as cantaloupe, citrus fruits, mangoes, and berries are high in vitamin C and tasty when eaten fresh.

VITAMIN D

Vitamin D is a fat-soluble vitamin that is essential for growing and maintaining healthy bones. Vitamin D helps the body absorb calcium, the mineral that makes up bones. It also performs other jobs throughout the body. It promotes healthy muscles, supports the immune system, and helps the nervous system carry messages. Vitamin D also may help protect against some types of cancer.

The body makes vitamin D when the skin is directly exposed to sunlight. People who

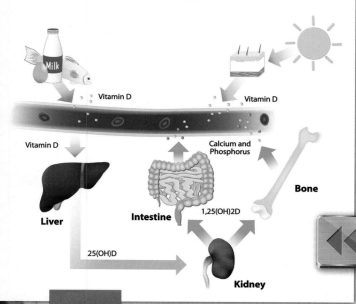

VITAMIN D

Milk

Vitamin D

Vitamin D

Vitamin D

Calcium and
Phosphorus

Bone

Liver

Intestine

1,25(OH)2D

25(OH)D

Kidney

The body can produce vitamin D when it receives direct sunlight. People also can get vitamin D through the food they eat.

Egg yolks and some fish naturally contain vitamin D. Most food sources of vitamin D—milk, for example—have the vitamin added to them.

experience little sun exposure and people with dark skin may not produce enough vitamin D for the body's needs. Therefore, it is important to get vitamin D through the diet, too.

THINK ABOUT IT

Can you explain why vitamin D is called the "sunshine vitamin"?

There are very few foods that naturally contain vitamin D. The best sources are certain types of fish, such as salmon and tuna. Most dietary vitamin D comes from foods with the vitamin added to them. These include milk and many cereals.

Vitamin E and Vitamin K

Vitamin E, a fat-soluble vitamin, functions mostly as an antioxidant in the body. It protects the cells of the body from damage that contributes to disease and aging. Scientists do not fully understand the role of vitamin E in the body. Good sources of vitamin E include vegetable oils, nuts, seeds, and green vegetables.

Many good sources of vitamin E, such as nuts, seeds, and avocados, also contain other nutrients.

Blueberries, which are sometimes called a "superfood" for their nutritional value, are a good source of vitamin K.

Vitamin K, another fat-soluble vitamin, enables blood to clot. Without vitamin K, even a small cut might not stop bleeding. Vitamin K is also important for bone health. There are two forms of vitamin K. Bacteria in the intestines make most of the vitamin K that people require. Plants also produce a form of vitamin K. Green leafy vegetables, vegetable oils, and certain fruits such as blueberries all provide vitamin K.

THINK ABOUT IT

Medicines called antibiotics can kill bacteria in the digestive system. Why might a long course of antibiotics decrease the amount of vitamin K being produced in the body?

THE B VITAMINS

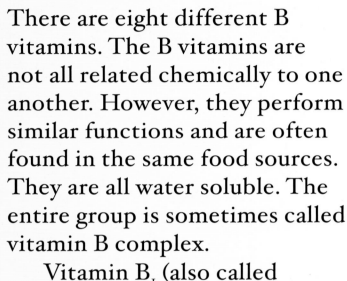

There are eight different B vitamins. The B vitamins are not all related chemically to one another. However, they perform similar functions and are often found in the same food sources. They are all water soluble. The entire group is sometimes called vitamin B complex.

Vitamin B_1 (also called thiamin), vitamin B_2 (riboflavin), and vitamin B_3 (niacin) are all involved in the **metabolism** of carbohydrates. This means

B vitamins help the body to get energy from food that moves through the digestive system.

VOCABULARY

Metabolism is the combined chemical reactions that keep living cells healthy. The reactions involve building up or breaking down substances called molecules so a living body can get energy, grow, heal, and get rid of waste material.

that they help to break down carbohydrates and convert them into energy. They all play specific roles in supporting the healthy growth and function of certain cells in the body.

Vitamin B_{12} is found primarily in animal foods, including red meat. The vitamin is also added to some foods such as cereal.

Vitamin B$_6$ helps to metabolize proteins. It also plays many other important roles. It contributes to making some of the chemicals that transmit messages in the brain. Vitamin B$_6$ also supports the immune system.

Vitamin B$_9$ is more often called folic acid or folate. It is important in making DNA, a chemical found inside every

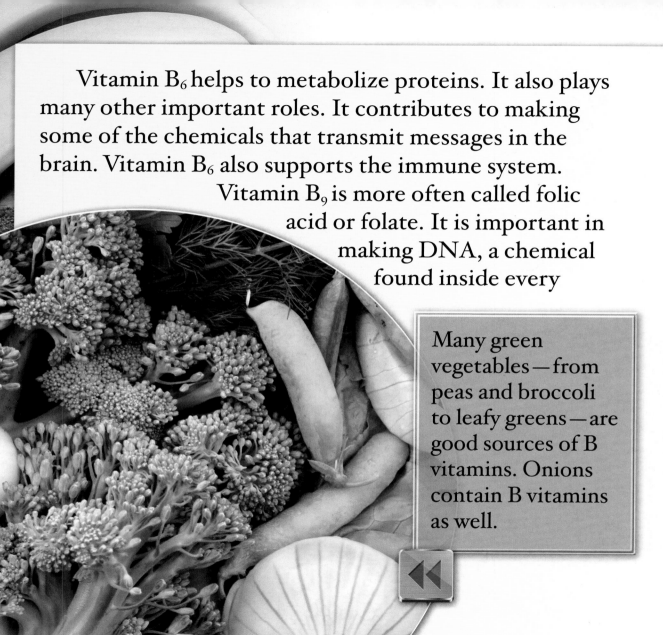

Many green vegetables—from peas and broccoli to leafy greens—are good sources of B vitamins. Onions contain B vitamins as well.

COMPARE AND CONTRAST

Some vegetarians eat dairy and eggs, while others, called vegans, consume no animal products. Which group should be more concerned about getting enough vitamin B_{12}?

cell. DNA carries information about a person's physical traits.

Vitamin B_{12} cooperates with folic acid in producing DNA. Vitamin B_{12} also helps to produce red blood cells and supports the nervous system. Unlike other B vitamins, vitamin B_{12} is found only in animal foods such as beef, fish, eggs, and dairy products.

Vitamin B_5 (pantothenic acid) and vitamin B_7 (biotin) both support metabolism. They are important for overall growth and good health.

B vitamins can be found in a variety of dietary sources. Foods that contain significant amounts of various B vitamins include green vegetables, whole grains, legumes, seeds, nuts, meat, fish, dairy products, and eggs.

Not Enough Vitamins

A vitamin deficiency, or a lack of an essential vitamin, can cause serious health problems. Deficiencies in certain vitamins result in specific diseases.

Vitamin A deficiency can lead to vision problems. An early sign of a vitamin A deficiency is night blindness—not being able to see in dim light or at night. Severe, lifelong vitamin A deficiency can cause lasting blindness. Other health effects include weak bones, very dry skin, and a weakened immune system.

One sign of vitamin A deficiency is night blindness. This condition is marked by poor vision in dim light or in darkness.

Scurvy, caused by vitamin C deficiency, can cause problems such as bleeding under the skin and poor healing of wounds.

Severe vitamin C deficiency can cause a disease called scurvy. Scurvy is marked by weakness, joint pain, and bleeding gums. In past centuries, sailors on long voyages often suffered from scurvy because they did not have access to fresh fruits and vegetables.

Vitamin D deficiency can result in a disease called rickets in children. This condition causes bone problems such as bowed legs and slow growth. Older adults with a vitamin D deficiency have a risk of bone problems such as osteoporosis, a condition where bones become weak and break easily.

THINK ABOUT IT

People of different ages require different amounts of vitamins, but kids should get as much vitamin D as adults. Why do you think vitamin D is so important for children's health?

Deficiencies of the B vitamins can cause several different diseases. Vitamin B_1 (thiamin) deficiency can cause beriberi. Symptoms include muscle weakness, tingling and numbness in fingers and toes, and mental symptoms such as confusion. A severe vitamin B_3 (niacin) deficiency can lead to pellagra, a possibly fatal disease. Diarrhea, dermatitis (skin problems), and dementia (a mental illness) are symptoms of pellagra. Folic acid

Rickets can cause bone deformities such as bowlegs in children who lack vitamin D.

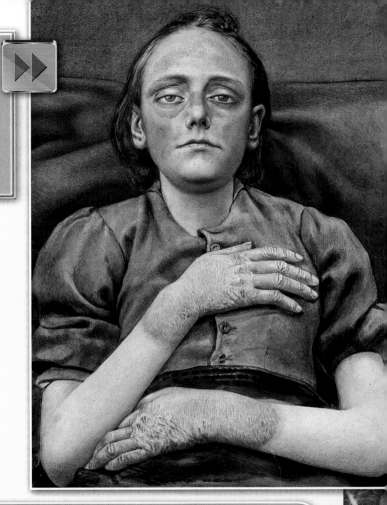

A painting shows a woman with pellagra. It is caused by vitamin B$_3$ deficiency and marked by a reddened scaly rash.

deficiency and vitamin B$_{12}$ deficiency often cause similar symptoms. They both can result in a type of **anemia** that leaves people feeling weak and tired. Vitamin B$_{12}$ deficiency also can cause problems with the nervous system.

VOCABULARY

Anemia is a condition in which a person has fewer red blood cells than normal. It can lead to weakness, pale skin, shortness of breath, and an uneven heartbeat.

OVERDOING VITAMINS

For some vitamins, doses above the recommended level can be dangerous. This danger is especially true of fat-soluble vitamins, which can be stored in the body. If large amounts build up, they can lead to **toxicity**. In general, children are more vulnerable to vitamin overdose than adults.

VOCABULARY

Vitamin **toxicity** is a condition in which a person develops harmful symptoms as a result of taking large doses of vitamins.

Even if a children's vitamin looks like candy, kids should not take more than the recommended dose.

Some people take big doses of vitamin C to stay healthy, but this habit can cause stomach problems.

Too much vitamin A can cause stomach distress, unhealthy skin and hair, bone pain, headaches, and blurred vision. Liver damage from vitamin A toxicity can be permanent. Too much vitamin D can cause weakness and nausea. An excess of vitamin D also can damage the kidneys.

Severe health problems from water-soluble vitamins are rare. But overdoses can have short-term consequences. For example, too much vitamin C can cause an upset stomach. Excess vitamin B_3 (niacin) causes reddened skin.

Vitamins and diet

Most people are able to get plenty of vitamins every day if they eat a healthy diet. Healthy meals should include a variety of nutritious foods. The amounts of vitamins required daily is very small. They are measured in units called milligrams or even micrograms. Trying new foods and combining them in different ways can make getting vitamins fun.

To prevent vitamin deficiencies, food companies sometimes add vitamins to products. This process is called food fortification. Milk is fortified with vitamin D. Cereal is often fortified with a variety

Kids who eat a nutritious diet generally do not need to take vitamin supplements.

Nutrition facts labels on packaged foods show the nutrients contained per serving, including the vitamin amounts.

of vitamins and minerals. The nutritional information on a food label shows the amounts of vitamins found in the food, both naturally occurring and fortified. Online government databases list the nutrients in thousands of different foods.

Nutrition Facts

8 servings per container

Serving size	2/3 cup (55g)

Amount per serving

Calories	**230**

	% Daily Value*
Total Fat 8g	**10%**
Saturated Fat 1g	**5%**
Trans Fat 0g	
Cholesterol 0mg	**0%**
Sodium 160mg	**7%**
Total Carbohydrate 37g	**13%**
Dietary Fiber 4g	**14%**
Total Sugars 12g	
Includes 10g Added Sugars	**20%**
Protein 3g	
Vitamin D 2mcg	10%
Calcium 260mg	20%
Iron 8mg	45%
Potassium 235mg	6%

* The % Daily Value (DV) tells you how much a nutrient in a serving of food contributes to a daily diet. 2,000 calories a day is used for general nutrition advice.

THINK ABOUT IT

In the past, the disease pellagra, caused by a deficiency of niacin, was common in the United States. Since the mid-twentieth century, pellagra has become very rare. Why do you think that might be?

VITAMINS IN A PILL

People sometimes take vitamin supplements to make sure that they get enough vitamins. They may believe that extra vitamins will improve their health. Supplements come in different forms, including pills, chewables, liquids, and gummies. They may include a single vitamin or many vitamins packaged into a multivitamin.

Most healthy people do not need vitamin supplements. But certain people may have a higher risk of vitamin deficiency. People who restrict their diets, such as vegetarians, may have trouble getting the required levels of some vitamins. Some medications can

Vitamin supplements come in different forms, such as pills, chewables, liquids, and gummies.

COMPARE AND CONTRAST

What are the benefits of taking vitamin supplements? What are the possible problems?

make vitamins less effective. Women who are pregnant may need to take vitamin supplements to guarantee that babies are born healthy.

It is very rare for someone to overdose on vitamins through diet alone. Vitamin supplements, however, can provide huge doses in a single pill that could be harmful.

For some people, vitamin supplements or multivitamins may be recommended in addition to eating a healthy diet.

GLOSSARY

absorb To take in or swallow up.

cell One of the tiny units that are the basic building blocks of living things.

diet The food and drink that a person, animal, or group takes in.

disease An abnormal bodily condition that interferes with functioning and can usually be recognized by signs and symptoms.

fortification The act of making something stronger, or the addition of material to something for strengthening or improving it.

function The natural action of a part in a living thing.

immune system The parts of the body that protect it from foreign substances, such as germs.

legume A type of plant, such as a pea or bean plant, with seeds that grow in long cases called pods and are used for food.

mineral In nutrition, matter that is not plant or animal material, that is necessary for good health, and that is obtained from food.

muscle A body tissue consisting of long cells that can contract and produce movement.

nervous system The collection of nerves that send messages for controlling movement and feeling between the brain and the other parts of the body.

nutrients Substances that plants, animals, and people need to live and grow.

organ A part of a person, plant, or animal that consists of cells and tissues and is specialized to do a particular task.

overdose To take too much of a drug, medicine, or other substance at one time.

precursor A substance from which another substance is formed by natural processes.

reproductive system The body parts that allow animals to create babies.

restrict To place under limits as to use.

supplement Something that supplies what is needed or makes an addition.

tissue In the body, a mass or layer of cells, usually of one kind.

trait An inherited characteristic.

vulnerable Capable of being wounded; open to attack or damage.

For More Information

Books

Baggaley, Ann, Carrie Love, James Mitchem, and Fiona Hunter. *Are You What You Eat?* New York, NY: DK Publishing, 2015.

Gleisner, Jenna Lee. *My Body Needs Food*. Mankato, MN: Amicus High Interest, 2015.

Mitchem, James, and Carrie Love. *Eat Your Greens, Reds, Yellows, and Purples: Children's Cookbook*. New York, NY: DK Publishing, 2016.

Pelkki, Jane Sieving. *Healthy Eating*. New York, NY: Children's Press, 2017.

Reinke, Beth Bence, and Shahla Ray. *Nutrition Basics*. Minneapolis, MN: ABDO Publishing, 2016.

Salzmann, Mary Elizabeth. *Eat Your Vegetables! Healthy Eating Habits*. Minneapolis, MN: ABDO Publishing, 2015.

Sjonger, Rebecca. *How to Choose Foods Your Body Will Use*. New York, NY: Crabtree Publishing Company, 2016.

Websites

Go Life Science
https://www.golifescience.com/vitamins/
Facebook: @GoLifeScience

KidsHealth
http://kidshealth.org/en/kids/vitamin.html

MedlinePlus
https://medlineplus.gov/vitamins.html

PBS Learning Media
https://ny.pbslearningmedia.org/collection/fizzys-lunch-lab/1/#.WjGIqSOZOMI

US Department of Agriculture
ChooseMyPlate.gov
https://www.choosemyplate.gov/kids
Facebook and Twitter: @MyPlate

INDEX